Design   David West Children's Book Design
Illustrations   George Thompson
Picture Research   Emma Krikler

The publishers wish to thank Claire Robinson, Education Officer at London Zoo, for her assistance in the preparation of this book.

First published in the United States in 1991 by
Gloucester Press, 387 Park Avenue South, New York, NY 10016

Library of Congress Cataloging-in-Publication Data

Petty, Kate.
      Pandas / Kate Petty.
          p. cm. -- (Baby animals)
      Includes index.
      Summary: Describes a newborn giant panda as it grows, develops, and matures to the point of setting off to find its own territory.
        ISBN 0-531-17287-2
        1. Pandas--Infancy--Juvenile literature. (1. Pandas. 2. Animals--Infancy.) I. Title.
      II. Series: Petty, Kate. Baby animals.
      QL737.C214P47   1991
      599.74'443--dc20   90-45005
                                                                          CIP   AC

Contents

Pandas

Kate Petty

Gloucester Press
New York · London · Toronto · Sydney

The giant panda

Giant pandas live in the mountainous regions of central China. There are fewer than 1,000 giant pandas left, and their babies are very rare creatures indeed. Most of what we know about panda babies comes from studies made in zoos. The giant panda is closely related to the bear. One Chinese name describes it as a "cat-bear." Its thick black and white fur makes it difficult to see in its snowy home.

A giant panda has a rounder face than a bear and distinctive black and white markings.

A panda in its natural surroundings ▷

The mother panda

Pandas are solitary creatures. They rarely meet except in the spring when it is time for them to mate. Several males might have a noisy fight over a female, though they don't hurt each other. The mother panda is ready to give birth early in the autumn. She makes a rough den in the bamboo where one or two *tiny* cubs are born. The babies are the size of kittens and have a similar mewing cry.

The newborn cub weighs less than 4 oz – its mother weighs about 220 lb.

The newborn panda looks similar to a white rat. ▷

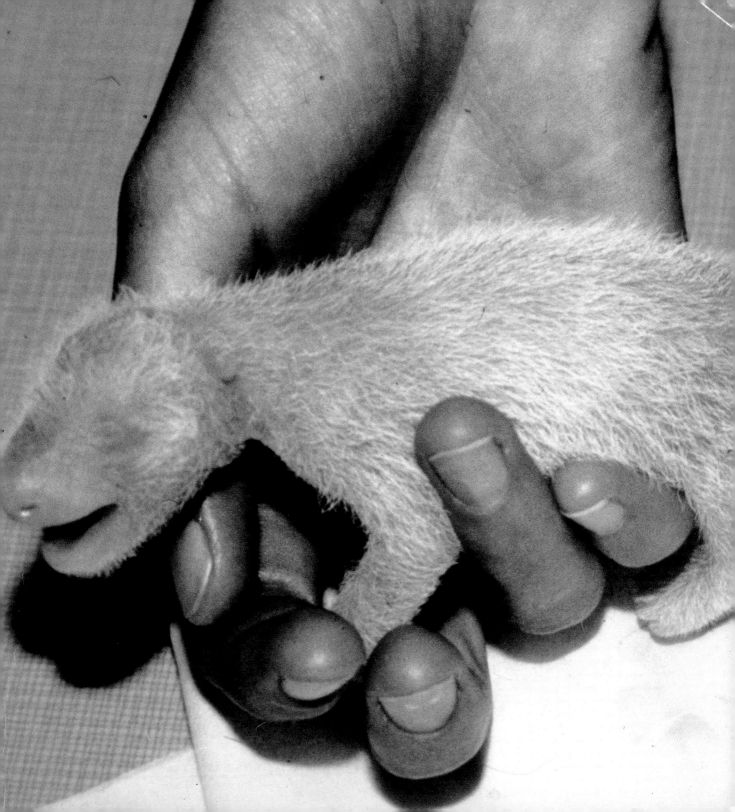

Early days

The mother panda takes excellent care of her cub, but she is only able to look after one. If she has twins, one almost certainly dies. The mother holds the little cub close to her warm body all the time, even when she sleeps. She suckles it every hour of the day. After nearly a week the black panda markings start to show in its fur. The long tail it was born with shortens and the fur grows thicker.

The cub soon starts to look more like a panda.

The four-week-old cub is already ten times its birth weight. ▷

Out of the den

The cub's eyes do not open until it is nearly two months old. Now the mother can take it with her when she leaves the den. Because the cub cannot walk, she carries it in her arms, or in her mouth if she needs to make a quick getaway. When she puts the cub down for a while, it rolls around on its back and waves its paws in the air, as helpless as a human baby.

At two months the cub is still too young to move about by itself.

Even at five months old a cub enjoys a good roll. ▷

First steps

The mother panda spends many hours playing with her baby. The play helps it grow stronger every day. At three months the cub is able to shuffle about in a sort of crawl. Its first teeth start to come through at about this age, too. By the time it is five months old the cub has learned to walk properly.

This panda is just beginning to get around on its own.

A mother panda cuddles with her six-month-old baby.▷

Eating

For nearly half a year the panda cub lives off its mother's milk alone. Now it is time to learn to eat bamboo. In the wild a panda's diet consists chiefly of bamboo – the stems, the leaves and the shoots. The giant panda sits up to eat. It grips the bamboo with an extra "thumb" that it has on each forepaw. A panda has to spend 14 hours a day eating bamboo to get enough nourishment for its large body.

A panda's teeth are flat for grinding bamboo.

The cub gets a lesson in eating bamboo. ▷

On the move

As soon as it can walk steadily the cub follows its mother on foot. Pandas walk slowly. If they need to escape from an enemy they will swim across a river or climb a tree. Pandas are very good at climbing *up* trees – they grip the trunk with the claws on their forepaws. They are not so good at climbing *down*. They come down head first and sometimes land with a bump.

Pandas are good swimmers.

A panda might climb a tree to get honey from a bees' nest. ▷

Playtime

Both young and old pandas are very playful creatures and seem to enjoy playing for its own sake. They tumble about like clowning acrobats. Pandas in zoos have to be provided with all kinds of toys to prevent them from becoming bored. Pandas particularly like to play in the snow, rolling around and jumping about in it. The mother continues to play with her cub, even when it is quite big.

Tumbling pandas

A panda plays with a log at Madrid zoo. ▷

Learning

Although the mother will protect her cub for many months, the one-year-old must start learning to be independent. The cub now weighs 90 lb and its second teeth have come through. It no longer drinks milk from its mother. She concentrates on feeding herself now, so the cub must learn to find its own bamboo shoots, roots and honey, and even to kill a fish or a bamboo rat.

The one-year-old's fur becomes less woolly.

The cub learns to find its own food. ▷

Leaving home

The young panda is fully grown toward the end of its second year. It is over 220 lb in weight and about five and a half feet tall when it stands upright. It is time to leave its mother and mark out a territory for itself. The home range of a panda covers about 1,500 acres. If a male panda smells another's scent on a tree or a rock he knows to keep away. The young pandas won't mate until they are four or five years old.

A panda leaves its scent on a tree to mark its territory.

The fully grown panda lives alone. ▷

Giant panda facts

Giant pandas from China are among the world's largest mammals. They are very shy and very rare. The mother rears a single cub that grows from 4 oz at birth to 90 lb at one year and 220–330 lb when it is fully grown. Nobody knows how long pandas live in the wild, but in captivity they can live to be 20 years old.

Baby

Adult female

Adult male

Index

Photographic Credits:
Cover and pages 17: Frank Lane Picture Agency; page 5: John
Knight Madrid Zoo; page 7: Rex Features; pages 9 and 21:
Topham Photo Library; page 11: L. Dominguez Madrid Zoo;
page 13: Robert Harding Photo Library; pages 15, 19 and 23:
Bruce Coleman Photo Library.